samoa

Pacific Pride

samoa

To Dear Molly + Bob.
" Samoa 2003 "
best wishes
and love
Lausi Niel Elle
Ross
x Max

photographs

Evotia Tamua

text

Graeme Lay

Tony Murrow & Malama Meleisea

pacific pride

© 2000 Pasifika Press Ltd
Postal address: PO Box 68446,
Newton, Auckland 1,
Aotearoa/New Zealand
Email: press@pasifika.co.nz

ISBN 0 908597 19 3

All photographs by Evotia Tamua except: by Robert Holding[†], Greg Semu[Δ], Dr Gerda Kroeber-Wolf[§], Stephan Beckers[Ω], Dr Ulf Beichle[+] and David J Herdrich[‡]. Historical photographs on pages 44, 47 & 53 are courtesy of the Alexander Turnbull Library, Wellington, New Zealand.

Consultants: Masiofo Fetaui Mata'afa, Fuimaono Dan Phineas, Pita u Taouma & Stan Sorensen.
Series Editor: Robert Holding
Design: Tony Murrow
Maps: Anna King
Printing: Acorn Press (Hong Kong)
Travel: Air New Zealand

contents

geography

Geographically, Samoa is thirteen tropical islands and their surrounding ocean located between 13 and 15 degrees latitude. Politically eight of these islands constitute the Independent State of Samoa, formerly Western Samoa. The remaining five islands are a United States territory called American Samoa. All of the islands were formed millions of years ago from volcanic activity. Far below the Pacific Ocean's surface two of the earth's giant crustal plates are in a long slow collision. One, the Pacific plate, is being gradually drawn westward under the other, the Indo-Australian plate. A by-product of this process, the release of molten lava (magma), has created a chain of high volcanic islands. Because the magma hotspots are pulled along by the crustal plates – in this case the westward moving Pacific plate – the islands of Samoa are geologically older in the east. Eruptions and outpourings of lava have occurred on the westernmost island, Savai'i, as recently as 1991. However, tiny Rose Atoll, 400 kilometres to the east of Savai'i, is so old that it has all but sunk under the weight of its old lava and the coral which has accumulated on it over many thousands of years.

The other islands of Samoa, stretching between Savai'i and Rose Atoll, are at intermediate stages of volcanic development. One of the younger islands, 'Upolu, is a mass of basaltic volcanic material. Its interior features mounds, craters and crater lakes, and peaks which are the remains of a line of formerly active volcanoes. Between Savai'i and 'Upolu, in the Apolima Strait, are Manono and Apolima, two volcanic islets. The Aliepata Islands – Nu'utele, Nu'ulua, Namu'a and Fanuatapu – are another cluster lying just to the east of 'Upolu.

Opposite: Piula Cave pool, 'Upolu.

1

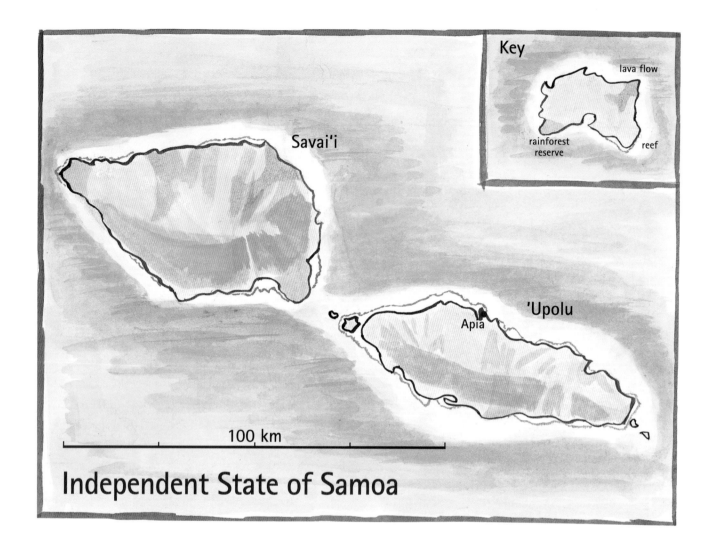

Key

lava flow

rainforest reserve

reef

Savai'i

'Upolu

Apia

100 km

Independent State of Samoa

The older islands have been greatly modified by erosion. Sun, rain and wind have turned lava into soil and sculpted coastlines into bays and promontories. This particularly occurs along the southern and eastern coasts where the sea is driven by the prevailing winds. Erosion of the interior mountains and the transport-ation and deposition of eroded materials by streams and rivers has created fertile alluvial plains on 'Upolu and Tutuila.

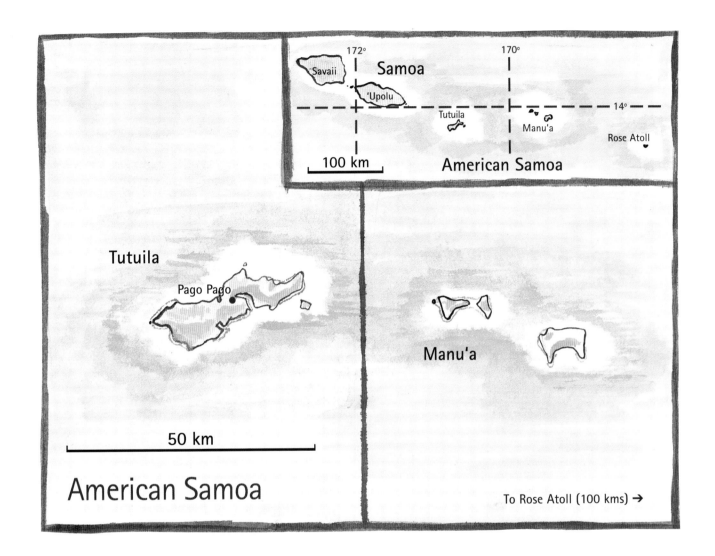

The effects of the erosion and the rise in sea level from a polar melt down more than ten thousand years ago can be most clearly seen on ancient Tutuila. Originally five andesitic volcanoes, the island's coastline is now heavily indented and the collapse of a caldera in its centre has caused the elongated island to be almost cut in two by the sea, creating the fine natural harbour of Pago Pago. The islands of the Manu'a group east of Tutuila – 'Ofu, Olosega and Ta'u – are also remnants of collapsed volcanic cones which have been eroded into peaks, ridges, bluffs and escarpments.

climate

climate Because they are so close to the equator, all thirteen islands experience constant high temperatures and humidity. Daytime temperatures average 26 to 27 degrees Celcius at sea level, but altitude reduces temperatures on the mountainous interiors in Savai'i and 'Upolu.

Rainfall is higher on these upland areas, and on the south and east coasts of the islands where the prevailing trade winds are deflected upwards by mountains and release the moisture they carry. The south-east trade winds prevail from May to November, bringing drier conditions during that time of year. December through to March is the wet season, when the trade winds are replaced by northwesterlies. Cyclones can occur at any time from November to April, when ocean temperatures are highest and depressions form in the Intertropical Convergence Zone, an area of converging trade winds ten degrees south of the equator that causes rising air currents and low air pressure.

The wettest parts of Samoa are the highest areas of Savai'i and Pago Pago, both of which receive a total rainfall of 5,000 mm annually. The relatively dry regions in the north-west of Savai'i and 'Upolu receive less than 2,500 mm per year. Humidity throughout all the islands averages 80%, but the effects of this are off-set in the months from April to November by the south-east trade winds.

Makerita Ekeroma-Brown swims in the pool beneath Papase'ea falls, near Apia.

Return to Paradise beach on the south-west coast of 'Upolu.

parks & reserves

Samoa has three large reserves – one on 'Upolu and two on Savai'i. These were created to protect and conserve the special ecosystems of the islands.

'O Le Pupu-Pu'e National Park is in the southern-central region of 'Upolu. Declared a national park in 1978, its 29 square kilometres have trails which lead to the lava tube cave of Peapea, through rich stands of rainforest and along the 'O Le Pupu lava coast. There is also a camping ground inside the park.

On Savai'i, near the township of Salelologa on the south-east coast, is a prominent volcanic landform called the Tafua Peninsula. Now a rainforest preserve,

5

A plantation road, 'Upolu.

Tafua has several craters formed from secondary volcanic eruptions, as well as stands of forest which are home to several native bird species and the endangered 'flying fox' or fruit bat. At the edge of the preserve, near Tafua village, there are spectacular blowholes, the result of the wind-blown sea surging up through fissures in the basalt rock.

Savai'i's other rainforest reserve is at Falealupo on the western tip of the island.

fauna & flora

The cloud forests of the larger islands – Savai'i, 'Upolu, 'Ofu, Olosega and Ta'u – host the most impressive flora in Samoa. The forests are of broadleaf evergreen trees which carry epiphytes in their sub-canopies and maintain a carpet of leaf litter, mosses and ferns on the forest floor below. Agriculture and logging have destroyed much of the forests of the lower slopes, but huge banyan trees are still common, standing like sentinels draped in their aerial roots.

Native land birds have also suffered at the hands of humans and introduced predators, but the upland forests are still home to the lupe (Pacific pigeon), the manutagi (crimson-crowned fruit dove), the sega (blue-crowned lorikeet), and the lulu (brown and white owl). There are also a number of bird species which are unique to Samoa: the manumea (tooth-billed or

6

Samoan pigeon), the puna'e (Samoan woodhen), the ti'otala (flat-billed kingfisher), the miti vao (Samoan triller), the mata papa'e (Samoan white-eye), the vasavasa (Samoan whistler), the tolaifatu (broadbill) and the se'u (fantail).

Naturally Samoa is visited by the many sea birds of the South Pacific. The Great Frigatebird (called 'atafa in Samoa), the white-tailed tropicbird (tava'e sina), a petrel known in Samoa as the ta'i'o, and the sooty tern (gogo uli) are all common and impressive sights. Another bird of the Pacific, the reef heron (matu'u) forages in the shallow waters around the islands.

Other splendid visitors include the pilot whale, but the most common and colourful form of wildlife is found beneath the sea. There are many beautiful tropical fish in the reefs and lagoons throughout Samoa.

The se'u (fantail) [+]

One of the prizes of the reef, the starfish, is often used as motif for siapo and pe'a.

7

The lupe or Pacific Pigeon (*Ducula pacifica*).[+]

The corals of Palolo Deep, near Apia.[+]

Few creatures other than birds, insects and fish have made the journey to Samoa's shores and found homes there. The islands, in geographical terms, are still very young and are some distance from the nearest continent where most mammals and other animals live. Geckos and skinks are common, however – the former are nocturnal and the latter live in the forests. A relatively recent immigrant, the Polynesian rat came with the earliest settlers – either by accident, as a food source or as companions to the Polynesian voyagers. It is still abundant throughout the islands. However, another mammal, the fruit bat or flying fox (pe'a), has been classed as endangered. Susceptable to cyclones, deforestation and introduced animals such as cats, dogs and pigs, it is now protected by law in Samoa.

The pe'a vao in flight[+]

The demise of the flying fox

There are three bat species in Samoa: pe'a vao (*Pteropus samoensis*), which feeds alone or in pairs on fruit and leaves; pe'a faitaulaga (*Pteropus tonganus*), which lives in colonies sharing a roost and tagiti (*Emballonura semicaudata*), the smallest, which roosts in caves. All are now protected.

The flying fox was once seen in large numbers early in the morning or at dusk, flying to feeding areas, but in Samoa 80% of the forest cover has been removed in recent times by cyclones and logging. This not only endangers the habitat of the bats, but the forest too, as many of the plant species depend on bats for pollination or seed dispersal. The flesh of the bat is considered a delicacy throughout the Pacific islands, particularly on Guam, which until the mid-1980s imported thousands of bat carcasses from Samoa to replace supplies of the Micronesian stock. Cyclones Ofa in 1990 and Val in 1991 wreaked havoc on Samoa's forest cover, destroying thousands of trees which afforded shelter to the three species of pe'a. Half the bat population was thought to have died as a result of the two cyclones, either shot by people, or killed by cats, dogs and pigs as the desperately hungry bats sought to feed on fallen fruit.

Efforts are now being made to conserve the remaining bat population. Two bat reserves have been established on Savai'i, and public education programmes set up to explain the plight of the bats and their importance to the life cycle of the forests.

9

The rough, lava-encrusted
coastline of southern Savai'i.

10

kilikiti

While many of the educational aspects of both independent and American Samoa are becoming increasingly Westernized, a few European traditions and pastimes have become significantly 'Samoanized'. Kilikiti is a unique South Pacific version of the English game of cricket, played by both men and women on the malae for recreation and between villages during the Teuila Festival in September. It is one of the best examples of the way a European element can be radically altered to suit Samoan needs and traditions.

Kilikiti differs from orthodox cricket in that there may be any number of players in a team, the ball is made from natural, hand-bound rubber and the bat resembles a three-sided club. The wood of the fau tree, which is light and strong, is used to make the kilikiti bat, which is also bound at the upper end with sennit. Bowlers bowl from alternate ends of the pitch, which is usually a strip

of concrete in the middle of the green. The bowlers and fielders are exhorted by their leader, who shouts, claps and gyrates in order to disconcert the batsmen. The batsmen must swing at every ball, and when they connect with it well, can send it high over the village green, the palm trees and the lagoon. When all the many batsmen are dismissed, the other team bats.

Kilikiti is exuberant, fast and often hilarious, producing fast bowlers, big hitters and dextrous fielding. Once begun, games can last for days, until the victorious team is found. One village at the eastern end of 'Upolu plays its matches on a spit of coral sand off-shore, increasing the chances of the fielding team running and falling into the sea. As pure, joyful entertainment, few sports match a friendly game of kilikiti, although the September championship matches are taken extremely seriously.

13

family & village life

Traditions are strongly maintained in Samoa. Many ideas and inventions from other parts of the world have been incorporated into day-to-day life, but fa'a Samoa – the Samoan way – readily absorbs these changes, and provides an environment which ensures cultural continuity.

Samoan children are born into the world of fa'a Samoa. A child's afterbirth, its fanua, is buried near the family home to link the infant with place and community. The family itself, the 'aiga, educates the child so that he or she has a direct relationship with both of these foundations. Traditionally, at the end of a person's life, they will be returned to the place of their birth for burial.

Opposite: children from Matatufu village carry water back to their home in the early evening light.

'aiga There are many inherent strengths in the Samoan extended family tradition. The 'aiga is a source of sustenance, certainty and comfort in times of social or economic difficulty. As long as the extended family is functioning, there is little need for child care centres or homes for the elderly. It is the primary unit of society in Samoa and the medium through which fa'a Samoa operates. Three or four generations usually live together or in close proximity, with aunties, uncles and cousins also maintaining ties with other family members. A child learns quickly where he or she fits in to this close communal structure by learning of the family's gafa or genealogy. Every member knows their place, their expectations and their duties. Those who carry out their duties know that they will be beneficiaries of the system in the long term.

15

Therefore, it is not sufficient simply to be born into the 'aiga; the child must also participate and contribute to the family in order to be fully a part of it. This enables children who show appropriate allegiance to the 'aiga, but are not directly related to it, to be adopted by the family. These responsibilities are carried throughout life.

In spite of the obvious advantages of the structure of the 'aiga, the burden of family obligations can be high. There is, for example, a distressingly high rate of youth suicide, particularly among young Samoan men. The cause is thought to be mainly the difficulties experienced by young people in meeting family expectations, and the conflicts between the young, who are often better educated in Western ways than their elders, who expect to be respected under fa'a Samoa.

Much is expected of young people and children are frequently disciplined with physical force. Older children are expected to protect their younger siblings. Brothers and sisters have a special relationship: a young man must maintain his sister's honour and a particular decorum must always be observed between the two. Young women are expected to preserve their virginity and to dress modestly.

Children are important participants in many ceremonies. On White Sunday, a Church day which celebrates childhood, young people are pampered by their 'aiga, dressed in their finest clothes and have elaborate feasts prepared in their honour. But children still have chores to perform and responsibilities to shoulder. This prepares the way for adult life and marriage.

The traditional Samoan wedding formalises the alliance between two families with an exchange of gifts. The groom's family provide foodstuffs, money and other products of male industry called 'oloa. These are exchanged with offerings made by the bride's family – fine mats, lavalava and siapo – all products of women's industry or toga. Such ceremonies clearly affirm the separate roles of men and women in Samoan society.

Status within Samoan society is very important, so craftspeople (tufuga) as well as village chiefs maintain a hierarchy based on respect earned through the performance of their duties.

Grandparents and other elderly members of the 'aiga are accorded great respect and authority (pule). They pass on genealogy, family stories, legends and beliefs, as well as taking care of young children while their parents

Maria Mataumu, with her daughter Maletina, runs a pancake stall at the old market in Apia.

are working. Fagogo (traditional stories) help to instil a moral sensibility in children and adults alike. These are usually told at night, and may be sung or accompanied with songs. Song and dance play important roles by fusing together the members of the 'aiga and the larger village community. The songs tell stories, mark notable events or express patriotism.

Most Samoans can say where both sides of their families come from and where they now live, even though emigration in recent times has taken many members of the 'aiga to distant parts such as Auckland, Sydney, Honolulu or Los Angeles. Weddings, funerals and other important family occasions are always acknowledged and have the effect of keeping the ties of family drawn tight.

17

Children from Falevao, 'Upolu village walk to school.

The 'aiga, then, is a complex and wide-reaching force. A strong example of the family's economic structure can be seen in the scale of the contributions made by expatriate Samoans in New Zealand, Australia and the United States of America to their extended families in Samoa. Overseas remittances (gifts of money) have long been a source of financial stability in Samoa. These are intended to compensate for any inability to contribute directly to the daily life of the 'aiga. Today many Samoans living in Western-style countries are feeling the impact of economic structures that are more individual than family in orientation. Samoans who are seen to withhold money and gifts from their families and are therefore unable to participate in the traditional Samoan economy are said to be fia Papalagi, 'wanting to live like a European'.

This is not to say that European ways have failed to have an impact on the Samoan way of life. For many generations Samoans wore little else but the tattoo and the lavalava, a cloth originally made from tapa and tied about the waist. Missionary prudery ended this. Today women especially are expected to dress more modestly in public. Special events demand more elaborate regalia, such as those worn by the taupou or the siva dancer, and Sundays or other holy days are marked with white shirts, lavalavas and dresses. But, because the climate is so humid and hot, a lavalava and light shirt are everyday attire.

Muga Ola from Matatufu
weaves fine mats ('ie toga).

Ioane at play in the village.

health

Health is another area which has seen an accommodation of old and new. Both Samoas have Western-style hospitals and chemists, but ancient healing practices are also maintained. Traditionally health in Samoa is holistic. Aitu (spirits) were once said to be responsible for all illness. Herbal remedies were developed by foma'i (special healers) to counter the effects of common afflictions and are still used to treat injuries. Massage is also used to cure a number of minor ailments. Healers usually specialise in particular maladies and remain an important part of Samoan society.

Common Western illnesses, such as measles and influenza, undermined health in Samoa in the nineteenth and early twentieth centuries, but Western foods have had a marked effect on the Samoan diet, and 'fast food' – particularly in American Samoa – has not helped the overall level of fitness of the Samoan people. The introduction of cigarettes and alcohol have also had an impact on fitness.

food

Food is a significant part of the family economy, but it also has great cultural significance in Samoa. It is very much a part of fa'a Samoa and is seen as a contribution to the 'aiga or as a gift to the community. The distribution of particular foods at ceremonies is determined by social position and largesse. Taro, for example, must accompany all food given to a person of rank, and particular portions of a roasted pig (manufata) are allocated to persons of particular status. Corned beef and canned fish are also favoured gifts at almost any gathering.

Traditional foods are often cooked in an umu (earth-oven). Rocks are heated on an open fire and then covered with meat and vegetables. More rocks are placed on top. These are in turn covered with mats and sacks for insulation, and the food is left to cook for three or four hours. Large quantities of food can be prepared in this manner. Often whole pigs are roasted in umu.

As in most Pacific Island countries, seafood makes a significant contribution to the Samoan diet. Fishing, like the cultivation of taro, is traditionally a male task. Their vessels, small outrigger canoes called paopao, are built by special craftsmen: the tufuga fauva'a. Paopao are still made from the sturdy trunks of pu'a, or hernandia trees, although steel tools now speed up the carving process considerably. The tree trunks are hollowed out with adzes, planed smooth on the outside, fitted with an outrigger for stability and used to catch the fish which abound inside the lagoon and just outside the reef.

Above: a popular meal of fish in coconut milk with baked bananas.

Opposite: a fale with the cooking area to the right, Leauvaia village, 'Upolu.

21

nu'u

If the extended family is the core of Samoan society, then the village, or nu'u, is the mantle which surrounds that core. There are 362 villages in western Samoa, representing nearly 80% of the total population, the reverse of urban-rural proportions in contemporary European societies. Each village has a distinctive history and identity which it takes great care to maintain, and loyalty to one's village, as well as one's 'aiga, is an almost sacred obligation.

The pride and care with which Samoan villages are kept means that they comprise some of the most beautiful sights in the South Pacific. Most are located beside the sea and gleaming white coral sand often surrounds the fale (houses), along with frangipani trees in bloom, huge mango trees, towering coconut palms and paths lined with white-painted rocks and colourful crotons. Imposing churches are also an integral feature of the village landscape. Such villages, which remain little-influenced by Western cultures, are most commonly found away from Apia, on the eastern and southern coasts of 'Upolu and, most notably, on the spectacular eastern coast of Savai'i.

Although the configuration of each village varies, there are certain elements common to all. The malae, the sacred central open space of the village, is the shared property of the nu'u. Fale are sited around the malae. These are the traditional family houses of Samoa. A fale, is oval-shaped and built on a foundation of concrete or coral rock, its roof thatched with woven

palm fronds. The walls, supported by posts, are open-sided to allow cooling breezes to pass through, but woven coconut leaf blinds that hang around the sides of the fale can be let down to keep out the rain. Fale are thus practical as well as stylish.

Fale contain little furniture. People sleep on mats of woven pandanus which are rolled up by day, although clothes are usually kept in pusa (wooden chests), and even completely traditional fale may contain a video

Above: a vigil is held for a recently deceased family member in the 'aiga's fale, Matatufu village, 'Upolu.

Top right: a family prepares food in the kitchen fale for the funeral guests.

Right: the intricate roof beam structure of a traditional fale, Savai'i.

Tala, a fa'afafine, runs a small store in Apia.

There are many special family roles in Samoan culture. One of these is the fa'afafine, men who usually dress in the same manner as and perform similar tasks to the women of the 'aiga. Traditionally they are carers of the 'aiga. Similar roles occur throughout Polynesia. Absorption of Western concepts of gender has complicated the place of fa'afafine in modern society, particularly in the more Anglo-Saxon influenced cultures of New Zealand, Australia and the United States of America where large Samoan communities reside. Both Samoas have annual fa'afafine beauty contests which are hugely popular.

and television set. Meals are prepared outside or in a smaller 'kitchen fale' near the main family home.

Nowadays, although the shape of the fale remains oval, modern building materials such as iron are commonly used for roofing and sheets of nylon cloth are hung at the walls to exclude the rain. Many villages now include Palagi-style houses as well as traditional fale. These non-traditional houses are built of concrete blocks or weatherboard, and have iron roofs and louvre windows.

Land-ownership in Samoa can cause difficulties, however, for while 'aiga are seen to be 'owners' of the fale they live in, plantations and forest-lands may be the property of an 'aiga whose members are scattered across the Pacific in cities as far apart as Auckland and Los Angeles, or the land may fall under the collective

ownership of the local nu'u. Conflict over land ownership can be bitter and protracted. Samoa has established the Land and Titles Court to settle these disputes.

The village's economic structure is an extension of the family's. Resources are shared, but in a more formalized manner. An 'aiga's or individual's place in the wider community is enhanced by an increased ability to share or give. This is evident in the relationship between all levels of Samoan society: between the individual and his or her 'aiga; between the 'aiga and the nu'u; between the nu'u and its larger district; and between each of the eleven ancient districts of Samoa and its respective government.

This complex system may place heavy financial and social demands on members of the nu'u. Because

Gift-giving is an essential part of Samoan life. Food is always welcome, particularly when large groups are attending functions.

Samoan culture values respect highly, competition for status in the community can place excessive strain on 'aiga or individuals. Still, in spite of social and economic changes in recent years, formal (sua) and informal gift-giving maintain the high-standard of traditional Samoan crafts, such as 'ie toga (fine mats) and siapo (tapa or bark cloth). Raw materials used in the production of craftwork remain entirely natural and are derived from forest trees and shrubs, as well as bone and shells.

crafts Samoan women spend long hours creating 'ie toga, fine mats made from tightly plaited leaves of the pandanus plant. The work is laborious. The long leaves are first cut, then stripped, soaked in sea water, washed and laid on the ground to dry in the sun. After this softening process is completed the curling leaves are sliced into thin strips and woven into the mats, which are used for a range of purposes according to their quality. 'Ie toga are presented as gifts of tribute on special occasions such as weddings, funerals or the elevation of a family member to matai status. They are items of beauty, symbols of dedication, and will last for many years. The women of the nu'u will also produce the mats that cover the fale floor for sleeping.

25

A paopao (outrigger canoe) is hewn from a tree trunk, painted and made ready for the ocean in just one day.

The other major craft work carried out by women is the making of tapa cloth, which in Samoa is called siapo. Siapo is made from the bark of the mulberry tree, the u'a. The fibrous bark is beaten into strips which are then glued together and decorated with traditional motifs. Siapo is used for decorative or presentation purposes.

Special craftspeople, who oversee the manufacture of such group-orientated products as siapo and fale, are known as tufuga. Male tufuga manufacture canoes (such as the paopao), supervise the building of fale, apply herbal or spiritual remedies, carve ornamental combs, orators' staffs, traditional weapons and so forth.

Fine mats and food are offered formally at Avoka Girls' School, 'Upolu.[†]

language & etiquette

Language is another means of differentiating status and roles in the community. Samoan is a Polynesian language which has two forms of speech: common or everyday language (tautala leaga) and the language of 'respect' (tautala lelei), used by matai. There are also a number of protocols that must be used when someone who is not a matai addresses a matai. The Samoan language is frequently supplemented with proverbial expressions that provide context and added meaning.

Village life observes a form of etiquette which is closely connected to fa'a Samoa and to the Christian beliefs which came to overlay it a century and a half ago. Most of these rules of conduct are common courtesies. Many have been part of Samoan tradition for centuries, particularly those involving speaking and sitting. One strictly observed protocol in most villages is the sa hour, the sacred times of day which are in early morning and late afternoon. During these two, hour-long periods, prayers are being said and heard, and it is considered extremely disrespectful to carry out any other activities.

village leaders/ matai

Traditional authority within the 'aiga is vested in the matai, the family leader. Each extended family has at least one matai at its head, a man, sometimes a woman, who is appointed through a combination of family and inheritance, and who represents the interests of the 'aiga at meetings of the fono, the village council. The matai is expected to strive for the 'aiga, to produce the maximum benefit for all members of the family. Matai command a great deal of respect and should be addressed by their titles, which include Afioga, Susuga and Tofa. The title of the wife of a high chief is Masiofo. The creation of a matai title is accompanied by much speech-making, celebration and gift-giving. In recent years there has been criticism of the number of matai titles being created, which is considered to be excessive. When the franchise to vote was extended to all adult western Samoans after the 1990 plebiscite, the provision remained that only matai could stand for election to parliament.

Matai are also responsible for the enforcement of village law and the punishment of family members who may have violated the social code. Transgressions include manslaughter or other violence, refusal to obey family orders, adultery or drunkenness, and punishments are often in the form of onerous tasks for minor offences or extreme humiliation for serious breaches of family protocol. The state also implements laws and punishments that are common throughout the Western world. Occasionally, the traditional and Western legal systems conflict with each other, but generally most offences are dealt with at the village level.

There are two types of matai: ali'i and tulafale. As we will see later, these distinctions have always existed in Samoa. Ali'i still inherit their titles and form an aristocracy of sorts. Tulafale achieve a similar social status by performing important administrative roles and showing excellence as orators. The tulafale's office is symbolised by the fue, a fly whisk made of sennit, which he or she carries when speaking officially. A to'oto'o or staff symbolising authority may also be carried.

Opposite: Utai Saalea, a matai, makes sennit rope and fue, the fly whisk used by orators.

the villagers

The untitled members of the nu'u are divided into four groups. The wives of matai are called faletua ma tausi. Children of school age are called tamaiti. Untitled men are collectively referred to as the 'aumaga and unmarried women form a group known as the aualuma (also known as the women's committee). These last two social units are the workers of the village. The 'aumaga is the nu'u's army, its horticultural division, its corps of cooks. The aualuma manufactures 'ie toga and siapo, it serves food and works behind the scenes when guests visit the village, and it supports health and education initiatives in the community. While matai administer and officiate at such events as the planting of crops or fono, the 'aumaga and aualuma carry out the necessary tasks which bring about these events.

In all villages the fale talimalo, the place where the fono or council meets, is prominent. The fale talimalo is usually in the centre of the village and is raised above the general level of the other buildings. The women's committee has responsibility for maintaining the fale talimalo, keeping it clean and decorating its surroundings with colourful flowers and plants. Before the fono meets, palm fronds are woven about the posts by the members of the aualuma.

The fono is comprised of all the matai of the 'aiga from the village and members are seated according to rank. All the important decisions relating to village life are made at the fono. Even the most powerful ali'i must win the full support of the other matai of the nu'u to make changes.

A sophisticated series of formal greetings called fa'alupega identifies the place and stature of those visiting from other villages or districts, so that outsiders can establish a formal relationship with 'aiga and the village. Often these formal greetings are accompanied by an 'ava ceremony.

Top left: moso'oi, fragrant flowers drying in the sunlight.

Top right: pandanus is dried before weaving can begin.

Bottom left: cocoa beans drying.

Bottom right: pancakes for sale at the old market in Apia.

ceremony

Samoan life is replete with ceremonies and gatherings, each requiring entertainment, communal involvement at every level, and respectful recognition of each person's place in the community ceremonies. Fiafia are particularly well-organised gatherings. Simpler affairs occur, but they too require song, dance and speeches. From time to time community members will go as a group 'on malaga', as a visiting party travelling from village to village. This will encourage feasting, discussion of political and social issues, help to arrange marriages, and provide the village with an opportunity to show its prowess as sportspeople with games of kilikiti and fautasi (longboat) races.

Fautasi (long boat) races in the harbour.

School girls run on to the malae
to start their dance at a fiafia.†

Fautasi crews train long and hard on the harbours of Apia and Pago Pago, preparing for the annual longboat racing championships, held during Samoa's Independence celebrations every June. The longboats are propelled by paddles wielded by young men and the races are contested in the usual, highly competitive Samoan spirit.

All festivals and competitions are accompanied with song and dance. Many of the ballads are joyful, some are laments, while songs expressing the singers' love for their homeland are always part of fiafia.

Fiafia are inter-village celebrations of traditional Samoan song and dance, carried out by men and women in elaborate costumes. The most common dance is the

Siva afi (the firedance) performed at the Kitano Tusitala hotel, Apia.

exuberant sasa, performed by lines of seated dancers. The sasa is accompanied by the beating of a wooden drum and has as its central performer the taupou, whose costume and headdress are adorned with mirrors and dyed feathers. The graceful siva is a legendary solo dance performed by a woman who narrates stories with the flowing, eloquent movements of her hands.

Often, the climax of the fiafia is the fire dance, a powerful display of courage and athleticism by a male dancer who performs with flaming brands in his hands.

The batons are tossed, caught and twirled, tracing fiery patterns above the darkened arena as the lightly-clad dancer leaps to the beat of the slit drum. Tradition says that only men who fear the flames will be burned while performing this spectacular feat.

In addition to traditional ceremonies of this type, several hotels in Apia regularly feature local singing groups, accompanied by guitarists and keyboard players. The standard of these artists is invariably impressive. Song-writing is a lively art form in Samoa, with some singer-writers skilfully blending traditional and modern themes in their work. Many Samoan singers record their work in New Zealand, selling it to the large Samoan community there and in Apia.

The other highly popular form of open musical expression is the brass band. No formal event is complete without a brass band performance. Most villages have their own band and, as with kilikiti, rugby and volleyball, competition between village bands is intense. The most visible brass band is Samoa's Police Band, which plays the national anthem rousing every week day at 7.50 in the morning in front of the office of the prime minister.

Today, however, the most common outlet for Samoan singing is in church. Even for visitors who are non-believers, a Sunday church visit is uplifting because of the sheer power and beauty of the massed singing. Just to pass by a Samoan church on Sunday is to be exposed to it, such is the volume reached by the congregation within. Nobody can fail to be moved by such singing.

Pinati, Kimber and Filipo from Saleufi at Mulivai Catholic Church.

religion Christianity has had a

marked impact on Samoa. Samoans have maintained links with their ancient beliefs through storytelling and song, but the new religion has found a place in the everyday lives of Samoans. The Christian ethos of sharing, for example, fits in neatly with the traditional gift-giving culture and the traditional concept of mana (dignity) is now synonymous with God-given grace.

The faife'au (pastor) is an important member of any Samoan community. He has the authority of a matai and his wife, like the wives of matai, is charged with organising events and educating children in the ways of the Church.

35

contemporary art & literature

Individually Samoans have made significant adaptations when confronted with the cultures of other nations, particularly Western culture. This is most evident in the new art and literature of the islands.

Although visual arts in traditional Samoa were confined to the patterns of the pe'a – the tattoo – and siapo or tapa, today Samoan artists have taken keenly to painting as an art form. Most of these painters live outside Samoa, however, where there is more opportunity for artistic training and more commercial outlets for their work. Some of the most exciting contemporary painters in New Zealand, for example, are Samoan. They include Fatu Feu'u, Michel Tuffery, John Ioane, Lily Laita and Andy Lelei, all of whom, though living in the palagi world, incorporate unmistakeably Pacific themes and patterns in their work. All, too, acknowledge the importance of their Samoan heritage. Prominent young Samoan-New Zealand photographers Greg Semu and Evotia Tamua have chosen the camera as their window on the Polynesian and palagi world.

Writing is another powerful form of artistic expression, but not one usually associated with an oral, family-based culture like that of fa'a Samoa. However, over the last twenty years a vigorous group of Samoan prose and verse writers has been published, both in Samoa and overseas. The leading Samoan writer is Albert Wendt, novelist, poet, short story writer and professor of English at the University of Auckland. But others such as poet Momoe Malietoa Von Reiche, Caroline Sinanvaiana, Sano Malifa and Emma Kruse Va'ai use both English and Samoan to interpret the world around them. Another woman writer, Sia Figiel, has published two internationally acclaimed novels.

performing arts are a
natural attraction for many Samoans. From the classics to comedy, performers such as Joseph Enari, the Black Grace Dance Company and Oscar Knightly are popular and highly professional.

Others are expressing their creativity and culture through the medium of film and television. Sima Urale received much acclaim for her short film 'O Le Tamaiti.

Opposite: "Tusi Pili" (1988) Michel Tuffery

tattoo/pe'a

One well-known Samoan skill is that possessed by the tufuga tatatau, who creates pe'a or tattoos. Although it is to some degree a prized sign of status, any adult member of the community can receive a pe'a if 'aiga, tufuga and village leaders agree that it is suitable. The full-bodied pe'a extends from the waist to just below the knees. The tufuga is commissioned with gifts of fine mats, food and other forms of wealth in the Samoan economy. Once the commission is accepted, the subject finds that tattooing is a prolonged and intensely painful process. As the tufuga tatatau works, his subject lies on the floor of the fale surrounded by other men who support him through the ordeal. Another man wipes away his blood and the surplus dye. It may take weeks for the pe'a to be completed. It is not uncommon for women to be tattooed, usually with a pe'a around the upper legs (malu), the wrist (taulima) or arm.

Getting a traditional Samoan tattoo – a pe'a – involves not only much preparatory ritual, it also requires extreme physical bravery on the part of the person receiving the tattoo.

38

The pe'a or full-body male tattoo.△

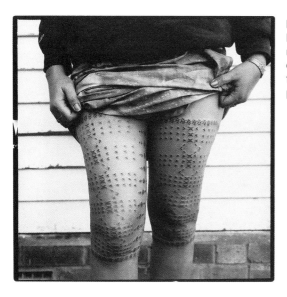

Left: women also have leg tattoos, called malu. Right: another example of a man's full-body tattoo or pe'a.[Δ]

the story of how the tattoo came to Samoa

Two women from Fiji journeyed to Samoa, singing as they went, 'Tattoo the women and not the men' – as was the custom in Fiji. When they arrived at Falealupo in Samoa, one of the women dived into the water to retrieve an attractive clam shell. When she was again seated with the other woman in their canoe, she asked, 'How does our song go?' Her companion answered, 'Tattoo the men and not the women.'

The two went on to Safotu village, and then to Salevavalu, claiming that they had skills to offer the Samoans, but not receiving the welcome they desired. At Safata, however, they were greeted warmly, and given siapo and the vegetable dye, curcuma yellow.

Right: the tools of the tattoo artist, the tufuga.[Ω]

Then the women showed the people of Safata their tattoo hammers and introduced tattooing to the people. But they instructed them to tattoo the men and not the women, because they could not properly remember their own song.

history

No one can say for certain how the islands of the Pacific were first populated, but many have tried to use what little evidence is available to chart the settlement of the region. Oral history, archaeology, knowledge of ocean and weather patterns, and the designs of modern Pacific islands canoes together provide insight into this process.

Some theorists have deduced that the first explorers were blown from the shores of the American continent by the prevailing westerly wind and found their way, by accident, to the 25,000 islands in the region.

More recent theories hold that the reverse was the case – that the islands were settled slowly, and to some extent purposefully, by those living on the western rim of the Pacific. This theory contends that human groups began to move from South-East Asia into Papua New Guinea 40,000 years ago and gradually moved east into the region now called Melanesia. These sailors 'island-hopped' their way to Fiji, seldom sailing out of sight of land for more than a day or two. At the edge of Melanesia, with the vast expanse of the central Pacific before them, these adventurers built great ocean-going canoes and, about 5,000 years ago, set forth into the wind. By sailing into the wind they found it easier to return from whence they had come, but it was also easier for them to move north and south. In this way the Polynesian voyagers found island groups as far apart as Hawai'i and New Zealand, as much through bravery and hard work as through their ability to 'read' the currents, winds and bird sightings which signposted their way across the sea. The migrants brought with them animals such as the pig and the dog and food crops such as taro.

Opposite: mats rest on a bench in the fale, Salani, 'Upolu.

41

Basalt waste flakes litter the ground at a prehistoric quarry near Tula, Tutuila Island.†

A prehistoric grinding stone for sharpening stone tools near a stream at Afao on Tutuila.†

These first settlers have been called the Lapita, named after the site in New Caledonia where a distinctively-patterned type of pottery was first unearthed by archaeologists. This type of pottery has subsequently been found from northern New Guinea through to Fiji, Tonga and Samoa, and dates from 1,500 BC. They lived on fish, pigs, chickens, dogs and rats, and grew food crops such as taro, yams, bananas, breadfruit and sugar-cane.

The Lapita people were the ancestors of the Tongans and the Samoans. The oldest known settlement site in Samoa is at Mulifanua at the western end of 'Upolu, a site scientifically dated at nearly 3,000 years old. This is among the oldest settlement sites in all Polynesia and is one reason for Samoa being referred to as 'the cradle of Polynesia', although older Lapita sites have been found in Tonga.

Near Mulifanua and on Savai'i are the remains of the earliest Samoan civilisation in the form of earth and stone monuments, some star-shaped, called tia 'ave. One such mound, Tia Seu on Savai'i, is the largest prehistoric monument in the Pacific, and although the significance of these remains has been lost, the fact that they required the coordination of labour suggests that they served purposes of dedication, either to a traditional ruler or a deity. No burial remains have been found within the so-called 'star mounds', adding to the belief that their function was mainly spiritual … although some speculate that the tia 'ave were used to snare pigeons.

politics & economics During this prehistoric era there were extensive contacts, peaceful and otherwise, between the Samoans, the Fijians and the Tongans, their neighbours to the west and south. In about 300 AD people from Samoa voyaged east to the Marquesas, from where there was further outward voyaging to Hawai'i, the Society Islands and Easter Island (Rapanui). Voyages fulfilled economic needs – trade, intermarriage and war. There are many legends and genealogies which record these contacts. In the tenth century AD Tongan warriors sailed to Samoa and settled there for many years, establishing themselves as a powerful force in the islands. The Tongan's eventually outstayed their welcome and were evicted from Samoa by Tuna and Fata. The Tongan ruler, Tu'i Tonga Tulatala, applauded their bravery, and in memory of this the brothers were given a title – Malietoa ('malie' means 'well done' and 'toa' is 'warrior'). However, they fought over the title and died as a result. Their brother Savea inherited the title and was known from then on as Malietoa Savea. A peace treaty called the Covenant of Tulatala was then drawn up between the Samoans and the Tongans. Although they withdrew their warriors, Tongans continued to become involved in Samoa politics for

many centuries. Until the time of the Tongan invasion, it was the small island group of Manu'a that held political authority over Samoa; its chiefs held the most important titles. But, after the defeat of the Tongans, the power moved to Savai'i and 'Upolu where Malietoa's kin were based.

Over the centuries, as villages engaged in economics and inter-marriage with one another, an array of chiefly titles had evolved. Eventually there were four vastly superior titles – the papa titles. In the late fifteenth century a woman held all four of these paramount titles, and for the first time all the Samoa Islands had an effective ruler. This leader was Salamasina and the new title of ruler of Samoa was called Tafa'ifa, the four-sided one (eluding to the four papa titles). Salamasina was a descendent of Malietoa Savea, but she was also related to the highly placed chiefs of Manu'a and the Tongan ruler, Tu'i Tonga. Today all the important chiefly genealogies can be traced back to her.

Before the arrival of the Europeans, Samoans grew food crops of taro, yams, bananas, breadfruit and coconuts, and hunted pigs, chickens and forest birds. Fish from the nearby lagoons and ocean were also plentiful. These abundant, nutritious food sources produced a tall, strong, healthy people. The most

prevalent disease was filariasis, which caused gross swelling of the limbs and was caused by a parasitic worm introduced into the bloodstream by mosquitoes. Population growth rate was surprisingly slow in traditional Samoa, the total number of people in 1830 being only about 50,000. No one knows why this was so, but certainly by this time Samoans had achieved a lifestyle of comfort that to some extent required sensible population controls.

In theory and, to a degree in practise, children inherited chiefly titles regardless of sex from either parent – although male leadership was the unstated norm. Then, as now, there were two types of chiefs in traditional Samoan society; the ali'i and the tulafale. Both were matai (chiefs) but each had different roles. The ali'i were sacred titles which carried with them the mana (authority) of the gods, as they went back to ancient genealogies. Tulafale did not depend upon sacred ancestry but carried special responsibilities such

Nineteenth century engraving of a matai.

as overseeing house-building, fishing, hunting or war. The ali'i made the important decisions in the community, after listening to the advice of the tulafale. All matai had authority over their extended families, the 'aiga, which in groups of between 10 and 30, made up village society. When either an ali'i or a tulafale died, senior family members would meet and decide which 'aiga member would succeed to the title, just as they do today.

There were three varieties of land in Samoa – the settlement or village area; family plantations; and uncultivated lands, mostly forests. Jurisdiction of land, naturally, ended at the seashore, but there were frequent disputes inland. The primary political unit was the nu'u or village. Each of these villages developed its own traditions and system of political organisation. Although wars between villages were common, villages and territories also became linked through inter-marriage. Ali'i had the right to give the name of one of their ancestresses to one of their daughters or sisters' daughters. These chosen young women were called taupou. There was intense competition between rival groups to obtain taupou for their chiefs in order to make important family connections through marriage. Taupou formalized inter-family alliances and inheritance in a way that polygamous marriage could not.

When wars were fought between villages, the fighting was carried out on battlegrounds away from settlements, so that mainly men were killed. Such wars may have also indirectly caused deaths, however, through the destruction of trees and plantations which were the main sources of food supply.

The only materials available for tools and weapons in pre-European times were stone, bone, shell and wood. Economic tasks were highly specialised. All the tools for hunting, fishing, cooking, agriculture and war were carved by men, who also carried out the tasks associated with crop-growing, building, hunting and fishing. Women wove mats, made tapa cloth and extracted the oil from coconuts. Cooking was done in an umu by the 'aumaga. Because of the abundance of food supplies there was ample leisure time for sport and ceremony. Early European visitors claimed they saw Samoan men and women with their hair made red by lime. Unmarried women shaved their foreheads and wore long side-locks. Sports included wrestling, pigeon-snaring, spear-throwing and slingshot-throwing; ceremonial events included 'ava ceremonies for chiefs, title conferring, weddings and funerals. Gift-giving was an important part of weddings, and consisted of fine mats, tapa and oil from the wife's family and food, pigs, bowls and canoes from the husband's family. As we have seen, a number of these customs are very much alive in Samoa.

Thunder, the protective atua of Amoa village, depicted in a print by Iosua Toafa.

spirituality

The pre-Christian Samoans were polytheists, worshippers of many gods, although they did not worship statues or idols as did other Polynesians, for example, the Cook Islanders, Marquesans or Tahitians. They had complex traditions concerning the origins of the world and their islands. These stories about the adventures and activities of the gods are still told today. Samoan priests, male and female, communicated with the gods, sometimes acting as spiritual mediums. They were then said to possess supernatural powers. Samoan ali'i were sacred chiefs, not a priestly class, and they believed that the powers of their gods and the spirits of their ancestors influenced human activities. The basis of chiefly respect was that the ali'i represented the ancestral gods of the family, village or district.

The Samoans believed there were two types of gods; the non-human – or atua – and those of human origin, aitu. Atua were superior to aitu. As was the case in several other Polynesian societies, the supreme atua was Tagaloa, who created the universe, earth and people. Great respect was accorded the elderly, in part because it was thought that people who died feeling anger towards their relatives would return as aitu, to punish the living.

A depiction of first contact, from La Perouse's expedition of 1787.

contact

Although by the eighteenth century Samoan society was strong, stable and long-standing, and although Samoan seafarers had ventured to many neighbouring island groups in Melanesia and other parts of Polynesia, Samoans had no knowledge of the world beyond the Pacific. It was their belief that the universe was a dome which ended at the horizon. Shortly a group of outlandish beings were to break through the dome and in so doing change the Samoan way of life forever.

47

After the Pacific Ocean was crossed for the first time in 1522, by Spanish ships commanded by the Portuguese explorer Ferdinand Magellan (1480-1521), the European world became intensely interested in the Pacific region and its economic prospects. Spanish, Dutch, English and French explorers sailed into the ocean over the next 250 years, to chart the islands and to claim them as their own.

The first of these European explorers known to have seen Samoa was Jacob Roggeveen (1659-1729), a Dutchman who sailed into the Pacific in 1721 seeking Terra Australis Incognita, the mythical Great Southern

Continent. Roggeveen sighted the Manu'a islands in 1722 and anchored off Ta'u, where he exchanged beads and mirrors for food. In 1768 the French explorer Louis-Antoine de Bougainville (1729-1811) also sighted Samoa and named them the Navigator Islands, because he came across Samoans sailing their canoes far from their island home and assumed that they must have had good knowledge of navigation techniques to do so.

In 1787 another Frenchman, Jean-François de Galaup Comte de la Pérouse (1741-1788), landed on Tutuila. A dispute arose between the Samoans and the French, and at least one Samoan was manhandled by the Europeans. This was a relatively minor incident in itself, but the next day a group of Samoans (possibly from a rival village) attacked the French while they were taking water on board their ship. This was seen as a retaliation for the dispute of the day before. Twelve Frenchmen and 39 Samoans were killed before the French hastily departed. Four years later a British ship, the *Pandora*, called at Samoa during a voyage to find and apprehend the Bounty mutineers. The *Pandora* was also attacked off the coast of Tutuila and again, many Samoans were killed.

Through these encounters the Samoans were made dramatically aware of the power of firearms. They gave the Europeans the name Papalagi, which means 'sky-breakers' or 'to burst through the heavens', as the newcomers had apparently broken through the dome which marked the limit of the human universe. For their part, the Europeans considered the Samoa islands hostile territory after the experiences of La Pérouse and the *Pandora*, and avoided them until the beginning of the nineteenth century.

The first Europeans to settle in Samoa were escaped convicts from Australia and sailors who had 'jumped ship', usually from whaling vessels which had begun to call at the islands for supplies. By the 1820s there were quite a few such men, called 'beachcombers' by Europeans. Some were violent and untrustworthy, others peaceful and likeable. Several took Samoan wives and established themselves as traders. Some common Samoan surnames of today – Coffin, Hunkin, Stowers, Slade, Jennings – derive from the whalers of this period as their bloodlines became mixed with those of Samoan families. Sometimes sailors who deserted were captured by local people and returned to their ships in exchange for payment.

a new religion

By 1835 whaling ship captains were calling at Samoa regularly for provisions during voyages which could last up to four years. Such shore leave gave the sailors respite from the gruelling, dangerous hunt for whales and so made them less likely to mutiny. By the 1840s Apia was a popular provisioning port where sea captains were able to draw on ample supplies of fresh water and food. Even after the numbers of whales caught declined, from the 1840s onwards, Apia remained one of the most reliable provisioning ports.

However it was not whalers who had the strongest long-term influence on Samoan society, but Christian missionaries.

According to a Samoan legend the war goddess, Nafanua, prophesied that one day a new religion would come to Samoa and end the rule of the old gods. Certainly, with the coming of the Papalagi and their trade goods, the world was now being revealed as a hugely different place which required new religious explanations. During the 1820s some of the beachcombers who were Christian had begun to teach the Samoans about the gospels, but they were not trained missionaries. It was not until 1830, when two representatives of the London Missionary Society, John Williams and Charles Barff, landed on Savai'i, that the official conversion of the Samoans to Christianity began.

Several branches of Christianity were anxious to convert the people of the Pacific, and so the religious rivalries of Europe – Catholic versus Protestant, Church of England versus the 'non-conformists' – were transferred to Samoa. The Lotu Pope (the Catholics) came to Savai'i in 1845 and established a mission at Falealupo, and there were already 13,000 Wesleyans in Samoa by 1839. Later, in 1888, the Lotu Mamona (the Church of Jesus Christ of the Latter Day Saints) also became established in Samoa.

According to the great Pacific missionary John Williams, when a village decided to 'lotu', or convert, they would have a meeting with the missionary during which the creatures that were sacred to the villagers, certain birds, animals or fish that were thought to represent their ancestral aitu, were cooked and eaten. In this way the spirits of the creatures were so desecrated that they could never again be worshipped. The village would then build a church and a house for the teacher or pastor. Money was raised for the church's work by the sale of coconut oil or masoa (arrowroot starch). What the people gave to the church was made public, so families, villages and districts began to compete for the honour of giving most. Education also became a major force in the missionaries' conversion campaign. Church schools were established in the villages and in 1848 the New Testament was printed in Samoan to assist in Christian instruction.

The social changes brought about by the conversion of the Samoans to Christianity were far-reaching. They were based on the ideals of middle-class Victorian England, where the family unit was a nucleated one based on the husband as breadwinner and wife as home-maker. The idea that women – not young men – should do the cooking was encouraged. Industriousness

Opposite: church, Fagaloa Bay, 'Upolu.

was fostered through urging the Samoans to work for money, by selling their crops, so that they could then buy trade goods such as clothes, cooking pots and iron tools, and was reinforced by beliefs that heaven is the reward for those who work hard. The chiefs were no longer allowed to have multiple marriages and the sacred powers of the old chiefs were transferred to the church pastors. Although Samoan Christians still believed that their chiefs had divine authority, now that authority came from the Christian God and required the chief to follow His laws and set a Christian example to his family and village. Tattooing was discouraged and clothing codes radically changed. Shirts, dresses and cloaks replaced traditional dress, which sensibly in the heat, meant covering only the lower half of the body. The missionaries taught Christ's message of peace, which conflicted with the traditional duty of a chief to go to war for his village. For this reason pastors and catechists were asked not to take matai titles as it would cause divided loyalties.

The Samoans accepted the various branches of Christianity so readily that within fifty years it had become the strongest social and cultural force throughout the islands. In part this was because Christian practices were often used to support deeper cultural traditions such as rank in the village and in the family. This is still very much the case today in Samoa. The official motto of western Samoa is now 'Fa'avae i le Atua Samoa' – 'Samoa is founded on God'. Today the main denominations, in order of the numbers of their followers, are: Congregational Church (formerly the London Missionary Society), Roman Catholic, Methodist, Latter Day Saints (Mormons) and Seventh Day Adventists.

While Christian missionaries were converting Samoans village by village, other Europeans were taking a commercial interest in the island group. The three strongest world powers in the 1880s were Britain, Germany and the United States. All were rivals jostling each other for influence in the Pacific, particularly in the Samoa islands. Each nation had traders there – dealing mainly in copra and palm oil – who wanted their governments to exercise stricter control over the turbulent local population, which was undergoing a power struggle of its own. Coconut oil was used to make soap, medicines and other sensitive oil-based products, the nut fibre was used in furniture upholstery and coarse mats, and the remaining coconut meat could be used as stock feed in Europe. European settlers looking for commercial opportunities had begun to acquire land from the Samoans for plantation use, and the Samoans were using the money from such land sales to buy weapons for their civil wars. British, German and American consuls had been appointed in the 1830s to represent European interests, and in 1838 a code of laws was drawn up to regulate the behaviour of European settlers. Samoa was put under increasing pressure to create a formal government in much the same manner as Tonga's.

Warriors at their fortifications
near Apia in 1899.

conflict

In what was to become Western Samoa there were four families contending for supreme authority: Malietoa, Tupua Tamasese, Mata'afa and Tuimaleali'ifano, the last of whom possessed two of the four papa titles. Wars had broken out in the 1840s and '50s over disputed succession rights, but conflicts were now made much deadlier because guns and cannons were available to the Samoans. By the 1860s foreigners were increasingly numerous and influential, but there was no authority who could speak for all Samoa, only the paramount chiefs of each village and district. When Malietoa's supporters made plans for a confederation, or fa'atasiga, with Malietoa Laupepa as king, Malietoa Talavou's supporters set up a rival headquarters near Apia and declared that only he could be king. Battles between the groups ensued in the streets of Apia, in

Malietoa Laupepa

1869, and damage to European property was extensive. Samoans would group about Apia in order to avail themselves of European commerce and intercourse, although this centralization went against the longstanding Samoan traditions of village-based power.

The American naval fleet, now steam-powered, had great need of a sheltered, dependable mid-Pacific coaling station, a port for the refuelling of its ships. The most suitable harbour for this purpose was Pago Pago. In 1872 the US Navy ship *Narragansett* visited Pago Pago and its commander made an agreement with Chief Mauga of Tutuila for rights to the superb harbour in exchange for US 'protection'.

The United States' tentative aim had been to establish a colony in the South Pacific and the idea of a 'protectorate' – as opposed to simple 'protection' – offered a shrewd path to this end. The year after the *Narragansett's* arrival in Pago Pago Colonel A. B. Steinberger, serving as the official agent of the US government, drafted a constitution and bill of rights for the Samoas and set up a government whereby the arguing kings, Malietoa Laupepa and Tupua Pulepule, would serve alternate four year terms. Steinberger then severed his ties with the US government, became Premier of Samoa himself and began to make secret agreements with German commercial interests, particularly the firm Godeffroy and Sohn, which controlled most of the prime plantation land on 'Upolu.

The United States consul, Foster, had commerical interests in Samoa which conflicted with Steinberger's activities. He claimed that Steinberger had never been 'authorised' to establish an agreement between his country and the people of Samoa. The British and US consuls were angry at Steinberger's actions and powers, mostly for commercial reasons, and pressured Malietoa to have him deported to Fiji in 1876. This act, in turn, undermined Malietoa's authority among Samoans. The self-government scheme fell apart and again there were factions – Samoan and European – scrambling for authority, complicated by disputes over the sales of plantation land and ownership titles. For the next 25 years there were seemingly endless disputes caused by the Samoan chiefs struggling for supremacy and trade rivalries, jealousies and mistrust of each other by the European authorities. In 1888 fighting broke out again. Mata'afa went to war against his rival, Tamasese, who had laid claim to the paramount Tafa'ifa title without sufficient support from the title-conferring villages. The intensity of the fighting caused the European powers to send for naval support and set the scene for the extraordinary events of the following year.

By early 1889 seven warships from Britain, the United States and Germany were anchored in Apia harbour to reinforce the claims of each nation to authority over the Samoa islands. As fate would have it, on the night of March 16-17 a cyclone struck Apia.

Only the British Navy vessel HMS *Calliope* escaped the ferocious storm: she steamed from the harbour and rode out the cyclone in the open sea. The other six ships stubbornly and fatally stayed in harbour. Ninety-two German sailors drowned when their three ships – *Olga*, *Adler* and *Eber* – were sunk. Fifty-four Americans lost their lives when two of their three warships, *Vandalia* and *Trenton* were destroyed and the third, *Nipsic* was seriously damaged.

Tamasese Titimaea

55

Mata'afa Iosefo

The tragedy had an important consequence. It led to a series of diplomatic conferences culminating in the Berlin Treaty of 1889, which declared that an independent Samoa would come into being, ruled by a foreign-appointed Samoan king, and that the consuls of Britain, the United States and Germany would hold strong advisory authority. Malietoa Laupepa was appointed king by the Europeans, but his rule was continually challenged by Mata'afa, who many others – including the famous Scottish writer, Robert Louis Stevenson, now living on the mountainside above Apia – considered to be a much more suitable leader. Bitter fighting between the rival Samoan groups again broke out, in 1893, and guns from American and British warships shelled Apia and villages along the coast of 'Upolu, causing heavy loss of life and property damage. The old factions, in other words, were still active, including the European ones, and all that was clear was that another arrangement for rule would have to be made.

In December 1899 a new contract was drawn up between the three European powers, revoking the Berlin Treaty. In this breathtakingly sweeping agreement, control of the western islands was given to Germany and the eastern islands to the United States of America. Britain withdrew from the Samoan scene in exchange for Germany renouncing claims to other Pacific islands, including Tonga, over which Britain would now have external responsibility.

Abandoned mansion, once a school, from the early colonial period, Pago Pago.[†]

two Samoas 'German Samoa' existed from 1900 until 1914. The first governor of the colony was Wilhelm Solf, who identified closely with the interests of the large German plantation company Deutsche Handels und Plantagen Gesellschaft (DHPG), formerly Godeffroy and Sohn. Because of the scale of its operations and because Samoans were reluctant to abandon their own agriculture and lifestyle, DHPG brought in indentured labourers from Melanesia and China to work on its copra and cocoa plantations. These workers were employed under harsh, poorly-paid conditions. Isolated from their homelands, they were much easier to control as workers and as a social force – for example, Solf forbade Chinese and Melanesian contract labourers to marry or cohabit with Samoans. By 1914 there were 877 Melanesian and 2,184 Chinese labourers in German Samoa.

Namulau'ulu Lauaki Mamoe

Solf also set about the task of removing the centralized Samoan government based at Mulinu'u and replacing it with a German colonial administration. He did this by stealth, not force, creating administrative departments, cataloguing land claims and placing many immediate responsibilites back into the hands of district and village leaders. Solf also legally separated Samoans from non-Samoans, creating laws which dispossessed 'afakasi (mixed race) of their inherited rights to land. Mata'afa Iosefa remained titular leader of German Samoa, but Solf was the country's chief administrator. Supremacy of a foreign power, however, was never truly recognised by Samoans, who saw the Germans and the Americans as 'protectors' not administrators. This perception would change with the new century.

In 1908 the first organised Samoan resistance to European colonial rule began, with the establishment of the Mau a le Pule. 'Mau' means 'testimony', and in this sense meant that the movement represented a body of opinion critical of the German authorities. The group sought to gain more control for Samoans over what was no longer their country, and was led by Namulau'ulu Lauaki Mamoe, a famous tulafale from Savai'i whose village, Safotulafai, are bestowers of the important Malietoa title. When the German rulers were unresponsive to the demands of the Mau, tensions grew and ten Mau leaders, including Lauaki, were exiled to Saipan in Micronesia, another German colony. Lauaki perished on board a ship which was sent to bring him back to Samoa, but he is remembered today as the first leader of Samoa's independence movement.

New Zealand troops invade Apia at the start of World War I.

On 29 August 1914, just after the outbreak of war, a force of New Zealand soldiers sailed to western Samoa and annexed the islands, without violence, on the instructions of Britain. This was said to be the first capture of German territory in World War I. The British feared that a radio station built by the Germans on a hill behind Apia could have been used by them in the war for naval communications purposes. The New Zealand military occupation of western Samoa lasted until April 1920, and was under the command of an English-born New Zealand farmer, Colonel Robert Logan.

Logan's rule was marked by racial intolerance of the Samoans and the Chinese. Like Solf before him, he attempted to ban relationships between the two races, who had already begun to intermarry. Chinese labourers who had married Samoan women were sent back to their homelands, but their wives and children had to stay in Samoa. Logan committed an even worse misjudgement in 1918. In that year a new, virulent form of influenza swept the world, killing millions. The disease was brought to western Samoa on the SS *Talune*, which was carrying infected passengers. Logan's authorities allowed the *Talune* to berth in Apia without quarantine and the ill passengers disembarked. The 'flu spread quickly through the local population and became an epidemic. In contrast, American Samoa enforced its quarantine regulations and did not experience an outbreak of the disease. When the authorities in American Samoa offered medical assistance to western Samoa, Logan ignored the offer. Twenty-two per cent of western Samoa's population (8,500 people) died from the 'flu.

Under the post-World War I Treaty of Versailles settlement, western Samoa became a 'C' class mandate of New Zealand, making it a New Zealand territory. But from the time of the 'flu epidemic onwards, there was growing discontent among Samoans over the New Zealand administration. Most of the administrators were military men used to giving and receiving orders. They had no deep knowledge of Samoan culture and were suspicious of any moves towards local rule. Brigadier-General George Richardson, for example, who was made Administrator in 1923, thought of Samoans as backward children who would, under New Zealand's benevolent influence, gradually advance until they could live and act like Europeans. He had no concept of Samoans being proud of their own culture and wanting to retain it.

Taisi Olaf Frederick Nelson

Tupua Tamasese Lealofi III

mau The Mau movement gathered strength in the face of such official prejudice. Its leader was now Taisi Olaf Frederick Nelson — a wealthy 'afakasi businessman, whose father was Swedish and mother Samoan — Judge Gurr (an American) and A. G. Smyth (an Australian trader). The New Zealand administrators were antagonistic to the Mau, and deported the three leaders to New Zealand. Alfred Smyth returned to western Samoa after three year's banishment, on Saturday 28 December, 1929, a day that marked a turning point in Mau politics.

Members of the Mau marched through the streets of Apia to greet Smyth. Outside the administration building a group of armed New Zealand police tried to seize some men known to be wanted by the government. A fight followed and several shots were fired by the police, then a police machine-gun was fired directly into the unarmed crowd. Eleven people were killed, including the then Mau leader, Tupua Tamasese Lealofi III, who was shot as he tried to pacify his followers and died the next day. His dying words were: 'My blood has been spilt for Samoa. I am proud to give it. Do not dream of avenging it, as it was spilt in maintaining peace. If I die, peace must be maintained at any price.' The tragedy became known as Black Saturday.

New Zealand's response to the events was to send a warship, HMS *Dunedin*, which sailed into Apia harbour on 12 January 1930. Most Mau members went into hiding in the bush to avoid arrest, and the New Zealand forces raided Samoan houses in their efforts to find the men. Throughout this period of great tension, the Mau remained committed to non-violent non-cooperation.

In 1936 a Labour Government was elected for the first time in New Zealand. More sympathetic to the Mau's aspirations, it cancelled the banishment order against the leaders and returned them to Samoa. Relations between the New Zealand administration and the Samoans slowly improved, though the administrators themselves continued to be men of little imagination or sympathy towards Samoan culture and traditions. During World War II United States marines were stationed on 'Upolu, and built roads and an airport at Faleolo, the basis of a new communications era. When the war ended western Samoa became a Trust Territory of the newly-established United Nations, but was still administered by New Zealand.

Then, slowly, the New Zealand government and the people of western Samoa began preparations for Samoan self-government. In 1947 a council of state was established, consisting of the New Zealand High Commissioner, as president, and the two Samoans holding office as fautua (leading chief) to act in an advisory role. A legislative assembly was also established. In 1954 a constitutional convention was held, with all sectors of western Samoan society represented, to consider proposals for the shape of the country's political future.

In October 1957 the New Zealand Parliament passed the Samoa Amendment Act. This redefined the role of the high commissioner, redefined and enlarged the membership of the executive council, provided for the appointment of a leader of government business,

Fiame Mata'afa and New Zealand Prime Minister Keith Holyoake mark western Samoa's independence in 1962.

increased Samoan membership and in other ways prepared the ground for the passing of political authority from one group to the other. In 1959 a prime minister was appointed in place of the leader of government business and by the end of 1960 the Samoan Constitutional Convention had approved a draft constitution for an independent state of Western Samoa.

independence The Prime Minister,

Fiame Mata'afa, took the proposals to the United Nations in January, 1961. This led to a United Nations plebiscite on May 9, 1961. All adult citizens of western Samoa were asked whether they approved the constitution, and whether or not they wanted political independence on 1 January 1962. This was the first

61

Throughout the 1960s and 1970s Western Samoa was politically stable and joined the United Nations in 1976. But in 1982 there was a constitutional crisis which saw the country have three prime ministers; Tupuola Efi, Va'ai Kolone and Tofilau Eti. These difficulties were added to by a legal challenge to the system of matai voting. The Chief Justice ruled the system unconstitutional, but this was later overruled by the Court of Appeal. Also in 1982 the Privy Council ruled that all Western Samoans born between 1928 and 1949, and their children, were New Zealand citizens with full rights in New Zealand. After much controversy this ruling was effectively cancelled after an agreement was reached between the two governments.

By the late 1980s the issue of matai voting was again raised. A new generation of educated Samoans saw the system as undemocratic, with many matai titles being created and sometimes used to thwart the aspirations of people considered better trained to serve. A national referendum on the issue resulted in a narrow victory for those who sought a more direct voting system, and in 1990 a qualified form of universal suffrage was adopted whereby all adults could vote, but only matai could stand for election. Elections are held in this manner every three years.

Western Samoa's political stability was tested again in the mid-1990s by widespread protests at the government's proposal to introduce a 10% goods and services tax. Dissatisfaction over the proposed tax was based on the fact that it would penalise those on low incomes by immediately raising their cost of living when few could cope with such an increase. The

time that all adult Samoan people had had the chance to vote directly, rather than through the matai system. The result was an overwhelmingly postive response to both questions and the Constitution of Western Samoa became 'the supreme law of Western Samoa' at independence on 1 January 1962, when the nation became the first colonised Pacific Island country to achieve political autonomy.

The constitution adopted at independence provided for a head of state, called in Samoan, O le Ao o le Malo, to be elected by the legislative assembly for a five-year term. The Head of State is largely a symbolic title, although the office holder has the power to appoint or remove the Prime Minister and grant pardons. In 1962 two high-ranking chiefs, Tupua Tamasese and Malietoa Tanumafili II, were made joint head of state. In 1963 Tupua Tamasese died, leaving Malietoa Tanumafili II as sole Head of State.

government pressed ahead with its Value-Added Government Sales Tax (VAGST) legislation, prompting protest marches in the streets of Apia. The churches and some prominent community leaders supported the demonstrators, and two of the protest leaders were charged with sedition. After considerable controversy, the Supreme Court dismissed the charges against both men, but the VAGST came into law in 1994.

In July 1997 Western Samoa became the Independent State of Samoa.

American Samoa
After they were declared a territory of the United States in 1900, the eastern Samoan islands were placed under the jurisdiction of the US Department of the Navy and designated a naval station. The territory remained under naval administration until 1951, when it was transferred to the US Department of the Interior. In 1960 the territory's first constitution was approved by the local population. It contained a bill of rights, granted law-making authority to the territory's legislature and promised protection for the Samoan culture.

A programme of rapid economic and social development was officially begun in 1961, using funds voted by the US Congress. Governors of the territory were appointed from the United States until 1978, when American Samoan Peter Tali Coleman won the contest for the first elected governor. In 1984 A. P. Lutali, another local man, was elected governor. The current governor is Tauese P. F. Sunia and the congressman is F. H. Faleomavaega.

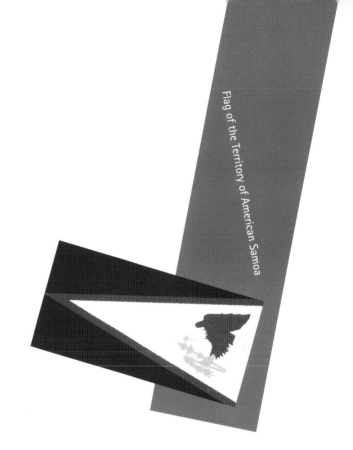

Flag of the Territory of American Samoa

Today American Samoa is described as an 'unincorporated and unorganised territory of the United States of America' because not all provisions of the US constitution apply to it. The governor is popularly elected every four years and exercises his authority under the direction of the US Secretary of the Interior. The territory looks to the mainland USA for its finance and popular culture, rather than the rest of the Pacific islands. The currency, national anthem and flag are those of the United States, although there is an official song, 'Amerika Samoa', and another, territorial flag which was adopted in 1960 along with the constitution.

63

ʻava

The powder and root of *Piper methysticum*.[Ω]

ʻAva, the ritual beverage of the Pacific, is consumed as an accompaniment to all important Samoan occasions such as a gathering of matai or a meeting of parliamentarians. The drink is made from the beaten root of the pepper plant, *Piper methysticum,* which is mixed with water, strained through fibre made from the inner bark of the fau plant, simply called the fau, and served in half a coconut shell. The muddy-coloured fluid is non-alcoholic, slightly numbing to the lips and if drunk in large quantities induces a mellow lethargy. Traditionally in Samoa the making of ʻava was carried out by the taupou, an unmarried woman chosen by an aliʻi as a social representative. It is distributed by a member of the ʻaumaga under the direction of a tulafale. Like so many other aspects of Samoan culture, the ʻava ceremony recognises status. Individuals receive the drink in order of their rank.

Above: an 'ava ceremony showing the 'ava roots (foreground) and the tanoa (background). Guests wait as the first cups are poured by the taupou, a young woman who officiates at these events.[§]

Tanoa are the containers which hold the ceremonial drink of Samoa. These 'ava bowls are the most common object of Samoan carving. Tufuga fashion them by hand from a solid block of the fine-grained ifilele wood. The inside is hollowed out with a chisel and the legs supporting the bowl chiselled out in one of a number of styles, from five single legs to five pairs.

Right: the tanoa.[§]

statehood

The modern states of both American and western Samoa show a marked awareness of traditional needs while also adopting many Western concepts. The Independent State of Samoa's parliament, for example, integrates a Westminister-style system with the traditional council (fono). This parliament – the Fale Fono – is located on the Mulinu'u peninsula, just outside Apia. The Fono is comprised of 47 elected representatives headed by a Speaker. There are two main political parties, the Christian Democrats and the Human Rights Protection Party. There are four courts: the Supreme Court, the Magistrate's Court, the Lands and Titles Court and the Court of Appeal. Local government includes administrative districts which oversee schooling and medical facilities, police and agricultural offices. Villages are still ruled by the matai system with these elected leaders meeting in the fono.

In American Samoa, a governor administers the territory under the authority of the United States Secretary of the Interior. There is a high court, a district court for each of the five judicial districts into which the islands are divided, a small claims court, a traffic court and a matai title court – the last three presided over by a Samoan judge. The chief justice and an associate justice are appointed by the Secretary of the Interior and district court judges are appointed by the Governor upon the recommendation of the chief justice and confirmed by the senate. The Office of Samoan Affairs, also known as the Office of Local Government, supervises agriculture, roading, water supplies, schools, sanitation and land disputes at the district, county and village level.

Opposite: a bus ride through Apia.

The children of Salelesi in their village primary school.

education

The European-style education system has also found its place in Samoan culture. A high standard of academic achievement is considered an important way to increase the social status of both students and their 'aiga. In economic terms education is also essential in western Samoa, where 60% of the population is under 20 years of age. This high proportion of young people puts a strain on educational resources and overcrowding in classrooms is a serious problem. Retaining well-trained and skilled teachers is also difficult in such conditions.

Before independence and for some time afterwards, secondary education was based on the New Zealand model, with imported curricula and teachers. Students sat the New Zealand School Certificate examination

Salelesi Primary School

and University Entrance. The curriculum has now been revised and a locally-based Samoan School Certificate examination is taken at the end of year 12 and a Pacific Senior School Certificate at the end of year 13. Most teachers are now Samoan and there is a training college for both primary and secondary teachers with enrolments of nearly 300 by the early 1990s. Outstanding students still have the opportunity, however, to obtain scholarships for secondary schooling in New Zealand.

The Education Department has overall responsibility for schooling, but there are also church-run schools which operate in conjunction with the department. Instruction is traditional in style and uniforms are mandatory in all schools. There are three divisions of schooling: primary, intermediate and secondary.

At the tertiary level, a technical institute offers vocational training in manual and office skills, and an agricultural branch of the University of the South Pacific (USP) is based at Alafua on the outskirts of Apia. This offers a degree course in agriculture as well as accommodating the USP's Institute for Research, Extension and Training in Agriculture. Alafua also offers diploma programmes.

The National University of Samoa was established in 1984 and offers degree courses in all major social science disciplines, including Samoan Studies, as well as diploma programmes in accounting, commerce and

69

mathematics, and a University Preparatory Year Programme Certificate.

The territory of American Samoa provides a wide range of educational institutions for the high proportion of the population – over 50% – under the age of 20, the result of a population growth rate of 3.7% in 1990.

There is no university in the territory but a government scholarship programme assists in sending suitable students to colleges and universities in the United States. Students enrolled at the Latter Day Saints college at Mapusaga also have the opportunity to attend Mormon universities elsewhere. Sporting scholarships occasionally enable American Samoans to pursue advanced studies on the United States 'mainland'.

sports

Samoans are ardent and skilled sportspeople. In several sports (rugby union, rugby league, netball, volleyball and basketball, for example) they have reached a high level internationally, including world rankings in rugby union and netball, a fine achievement for two small island territories with small populations. As well, expatriate Samoans have achieved distinction in their adopted lands, American Samoans playing gridiron football in the United States, and Samoan New Zealanders starring in national rugby and netball teams for New Zealand.

Below: the Independent State of Samoa's national rugby team Manu Samoa in a match against Fiji.

Above: a strenuous inter-village game of tug-of-war.

Inter-village competitions also feature sports such as kilikiti, boat racing and tug-of-war.

Rugby union is a passion in western Samoa, whether it is played on an impromptu basis on the beach or at an international level at Apia Park. Every village green sprouts rugby goalposts, some of which in turn sprout with foliage in the tropical climate. Boys and young men take every opportunity to set up a game and matches between villages and schools are vigorously contested. Rugby, a highly physical, body-contact sport, is seen as an expression of Samoan manhood. From a small but extremely talented local pool, plus its overseas-based players, western Samoa's national rugby team, Manu Samoa, is selected for international competition. The team plays in an annual triangular tournament against neighbouring Fiji and Tonga, and has had some remarkable performances in Rugby World Cup tournaments, earning respect for its style and spirit.

Rugby league has gained strength in western Samoa in recent years, its hard-running, hard-tackling style of play also suiting Samoan tastes. League also offers the incentive of payments to players. Many leading league players in New Zealand and Australia are originally from western Samoa.

Speed, dexterity and teamwork are the qualities of a top netballer, and western Samoa possesses a large number of women with such attributes. As with rugby,

71

many of New Zealand's outstanding netballers of recent times have been Samoan, including Rita Fatialofa, April Ieremia and Bernice Mene. Volleyball is second only to netball in popularity among Samoan women, and the standard of play in this fast ball sport is uniformly high.

Beatrice Faumuina acheived international fame by winning a gold medal at the 1998 Commonwealth Games for the shot put.

Sport in American Samoa reflects the preferences of mainland Unites States. Live television coverage of baseball and American football has fostered the popularity of those sports, which are played with enthuiasm at a high level of proficiency.

economy
While Samoans have adapted to and modified many Western ideas and devices to their own ends, some introduced concepts undermine traditional values and bring pressures on the communities of the islands. Economic change is an example of this. Samoa's gift-giving economy, which extends from the family to the village and then on to inter-village activity, is not permitted to function quite so simply at a government level. Both states and the businesses that operate within them must engender the goodwill of other nations and foreign companies that

Below: coconuts on the Savai'i ferry.

survive on a cash-based economy. This means that both Samoas have two effective economies: a free market economy, and a barter or green economy.

At the time of independence in 1962 it was envisaged that western Samoa's traditionally agriculture-based way of life would undergo a steady transformation to a cash economy based on commercial agriculture, supplemented by a modern infrastructure including shipping and aviation, and assisted by foreign investment. Political leaders saw this development path as the most promising one and held up a vision of

Opposite: Faiala'a Iloilo in her roadside shop, Lotofaga village.

A local bus runs along the foreshore.

steady economic growth and development leading to increasing national prosperity. Several factors conspired to frustrate these hopes, however.

With a combination of a high birth rate and a greatly reduced death rate, population growth in the 1960s became extremely rapid, outstripping the ability of the economy to provide satisfactory employment and education for all. During the same period prices for important export crops such as copra and cocoa dropped sharply and the banana crop was struck by disease, giving little incentive for small-scale cultivators to expand their operations. The cost of living increased, there was a drift of population to the capital, Apia, but what little work there was in the town was poorly paid.

In 1966 a cyclone ravaged crops and buildings, and killed ten people. The international community sent food relief in the form of rice, flour, tinned fish and meat and dried eggs and milk. The people developed a preference for these processed food imports, which were of dubious nutritional value, and this led to a further decline in traditional agriculture and fishing.

For those western Samoans with ambitions for themselves and their children, emigration seemed more and more to be the logical option. During 1964 and 1965 over 2,000 western Samoans went to New Zealand to work on three month or six month visas. Because of the Treaty of Friendship signed between western Samoa and New Zealand at the time of independence, there was no need for these migrants to register as 'aliens' in New Zealand, where there was then plenty of relatively well-paid factory work available. The pace of emigration quickened through the later 1960s and early 1970s. Those already in New

Opposite (clockwise from top left):
Government Building, Apia;
Pago Pago, American Samoa;
The *Lady Samoa* is loaded in Apia
before its regular voyage to Savai'i.

Zealand workplaces arranged jobs for others of their 'aiga, who had to obtain an employer's guarantee before a visa was issued. By the early 1990s there were 66,000 people of western Samoan extraction living in New Zealand and, ironically, ties between the two countries became stronger than they had ever been during colonial rule.

Remittances from overseas-based Samoans became a significant source of income for those at home as a proportion of incomes earned in New Zealand or other migrant destinations such as the USA and Australia were sent back to members of the extended family still in Samoa. By 1991 these remittances accounted for $74.4 million. From 1984 to 1990 they comprised 29% of western Samoa's Gross Domestic Product (GDP). Although the remittances helped the balance of payments, the money was usually spent on imported consumer goods rather than being invested in more productive sectors of the economy. This aggravated inflation and slowed economic development.

75

Another major source of economic assistance after independence came from foreign aid, in the form of loans, grants or technical help. The aid donors include Japan, New Zealand, Australia, China, Germany, the United Nations Development Programme and the European Community. In 1990 the total value of aid to western Samoa was $44.3 million.

Development plans, particularly in agriculture, suffered two devastating blows in 1990 and 1991 when cyclones Ofa and Val struck the archipelago. The cyclones, only 21 months apart, stripped palm trees and caused salt spray damage to other plantation crops. Primary production, particularly of coconuts, was severely affected, and the production of coconut cream, the most important coconut extract, became dependent on imported nuts until the palm trees recovered. The value of coconut cream had surpassed that of another traditional crop, copra, by the early 1990s. Cocoa, a high-quality export product, also suffered from cyclone damage, as did taro, the staple food crop which was also exported to Samoan communities overseas. Taro growers suffered a further blow in 1994, when the crop was decimated by blight, removing a vital source of food and cash income for growers.

tourism A potentially

valuable source of foreign exchange and employment, tourism was slow to be developed after independence because many leaders thought that an influx of Papalagi tourists would threaten fa'a Samoa. Attitudes have now changed, however, and tourism is seen as a likely growth industry. Both Samoas have a number of fine

Polynesian Airlines operate some local services from Fagali'i Airport on 'Upolu.

attributes: a unique culture, extensive areas of unspoilt coastline, spectacular volcanic landscapes, rainforests, lakes and waterfalls and beautifully maintained villages provide manifest exotic attractions for overseas visitors, particularly those from Europe.

Tourism is a highly competitive industry however and requires the highest standards of transport, accommodation and service. There are two international-standard hotels in Apia, Aggie Grey's and Kitano Tusitala, along with several motels and guest houses of a good standard. Many villages on 'Upolu and Savai'i now rent traditional-style fales to tourists. These are located on the beach, providing elementary shelter in an idyllic setting for those who wish to experience village life at a budget price. Meals can also be provided by the villagers for these

Above: situated thirty minutes from Apia, Faleolo Airport is the gateway to western Samoa for most visitors.

tourists, should they require them. Other resorts, such as Stevenson's at Manase, on Savai'i's north coast, offer both beach-fale and resort accommodation; while the Safua Hotel in eastern Savai'i is justly renowned for introducing Samoan culture to its guests.

Apia contains a variety of businesses which cater to the needs of tourists as well as local people. These include gift shops, travel agents, tour companies, snack bars, restaurants, nightclubs and car rental firms. The large 'flea market' on the waterfront at the western end of Apia is one of the best in the Pacific Islands, offering a wide variety of clothes, toiletries and handicrafts at reasonable prices, and the new produce market behind central Apia sells fruit and vegetables fresh from the countryside.

Right: take the cablecar to the top of Rainmaker Mountain for a magnificent view of Pago Pago harbour.[†]

The Independent State of Samoa is served by four international airlines; Polynesian Airlines, Air New Zealand, Air Pacific and Samoa Air through Faleolo International Airport, 35 kilometres from Apia. There is an airstrip at Fagali'i in Apia, where flights leave daily for Savai'i, and Fagali'i also receives flights from American Samoa by Samoa Air and Polynesian Airlines. After an ambitious expansion programme in the early 1990s, which included routes to Tahiti, Hawai'i and Los Angeles, Polynesian Airlines sustained heavy losses, subsequently abandoned these routes and is now once again concentrating on serving its own region.

industry The manufacturing sector of western Samoa's economy is aimed at supplying the local market and consists of the processing of food products such as bread, biscuits, soft drinks, corned meat and ice cream. Other important industries are brewing of the local beer, Vailima, cigarette-making and building supplies such as timber and paint. A Japanese company, Yazaki Samoa Ltd, manufactures automotive electrical equipment for export to Australia. In dollar terms, this product now accounts for 82% of all western Samoa's exports.

Yet western Samoa faces considerable economic difficulties. Wage rates remain generally low, with a legal minimum adult wage rate of 43 US cents per hour, a rate for clerical workers of $2.40 per hour and for lower management, $5 per hour. GDP per capita in 1991 was $1,713. The balance of trade has steadily worsened over the last decade, with the cost of imports exceeding the value of exports by $200 million dollars in 1991. Foreign aid, remittances from Samoans living overseas and tourist revenue have helped redress this imbalance, but the double blow of cyclones Ofa and Val ravaging export crops in the early 1990s, and the taro blight of the mid-1990s have made recovery all the more difficult. On the other hand, the cyclones purged the islands of 'weak' crops, permitting stronger coconut palms and taro to flourish. The devastation has also afforded an opportunity for much-needed public works programs to begin.

Western Samoa now has an excellent roading system. Sealed, well-aligned roads pass through the most populated areas, in the northern districts of 'Upolu and Savai'i, and these arterial roads connect the many villages along the coastlines of both main islands. There are now only short sections of these main roads which are not sealed.

Concrete fords have been built where the roads cross the rivers which run down from the interior mountains, as these become torrents which can destroy bridges during periods of high rainfall. On 'Upolu there are two roads which cross the island from north to south, one near the western end and the other from Apia, but there are no roads which cross Savai'i from north to south.

A view of Apia from Mount Vaea, 'Upolu.

Public transport takes the form of distinctively large, brightly-painted Toyota buses that connect the villages with Apia and Salelologa on Savai'i. These windowless buses are all privately owned, their abundant decorations reflecting the tastes and interests of their drivers. Many of the villages depend on the bus to carry supplies of all kinds, as well as passengers, to remote districts where cars or utility trucks are rare. The density of motor vehicle traffic in Apia increased to such an extent that in 1994 traffic lights had to be installed at several key intersections. While these have regulated the traffic, the crowding, particularly along Beach Road, remains.

Apia's deepwater port has a large berthing facility and wharf, goods sheds, a mobile crane and forklifts to handle cargo. The large Pacific Forum Line is based in Apia and maintains shipping services between Samoa, other Pacific Islands, Australia and New Zealand.

Fagatogo township near Pago Pago, a commercial centre.

American Samoa's economy is closely tied to the public service, which is in turn tied to finance provided by the United States Congress. American Samoans are nationals of the United States with right of free entry to that country. After meeting the necessary requirements they may become citizens of the USA. Many have done so by serving in a branch of the United States Armed Services. Half the population of the territory works in the government sector. GDP per capita was $US4,450 in 1985, four and a half times the figure for western Samoa, and annual aid per capita from the USA is estimated at $US1,700.

The streets of Pago Pago, lined with the US and American Samoan flags.

80

Ferries take cargo and passengers between the islands and both Samoas.

Agriculture has declined sharply in recent years in American Samoa, partly as a result of cyclone damage, and partly because an alternative income and imported food are much more easily obtained elsewhere. All food crops produced are for local consumption, with taro the most common crop, followed by bananas, coconuts, paw paw and pineapples.

Fish canning is the territory's dominant industry, with two canneries located side by side at Satala, on the bay of Pago Pago. The canneries employ 4,300 workers, many of whom come from western Samoa. The tuna is supplied by fishing boats from the United States, Taiwan and Korea, which account for more than half the vessel movements in and out of Pago Pago harbour. In 1990 the value of the canned tuna, nearly all of which is sent to the United States, was $US306 million. This included a by-product of the cannery, pet-food. The only other industrial centre is at Tafuna, near the airport, where an industrial estate has been established.

Tourism is not well developed in American Samoa, mainly because of unreliable air connections with the US mainland and other parts of the Pacific. Some cruise ships call at Pago Pago for short visits. There is one sizeable hotel, the Rainmaker, but the naturally attractive harbour has been sullied by waste from the tuna canneries. In 1990 8,499 tourists visited American Samoa. The outer Manu'a islands remain unspoilt, however, and have the potential to attract tourists should a suitable infrastructure be established in the territory.

81

A twilight view of Pago Pago harbour.[†]

Communications are well developed on Tutuila, the main island in the territory of American Samoa, where many roads are now sealed. The major arterial road connects Pago Pago with the airport at Tafuna and there is a high ratio of private motor vehicles – 4,243 for the 35,000 inhabitants. Brightly painted buses equipped with loud stereo systems serve the rest of the population.

American Samoa has air links provided by Polynesian Airlines, Hawaiian Airlines and Air Nauru. The service between American Samoa and western Samoa by Polynesian Airlines and Samoa Air is helpful because it connects the territory with the more reliable airlines which serve other parts of the Pacific, as well as providing a service for the many Samoans with family members in the 'other' Samoa. There are small airstrips on two other islands in the Manu'a group, Ta'u and 'Ofu.

Sano Malifa, editor and owner of the *Samoa Observer* in his Apia office.

Pago Pago's sheltered harbour is its principal geographic and economic asset. Deep and virtually cyclone-proof because of its right-angled bend and surrounding mountains, the harbour is the focus of shipping services, fish processing industries and other commercial activities.

American Samoa has for many years enjoyed modern telecommunications with other countries, particularly the United States. Television broadcasts began as early as 1964. Today the system uses the COMSAT satellite network. There are also direct dial telephone and facsimile services readily available, while the postage rates and stamps used are the same as those on the United States mainland. An AM and an FM radio station broadcast programmes in both Samoan and English.

Three weekly newspapers are published in Pago Pago, printing local news in Samoan and English, and a wide variety of American news magazines are imported from the mainland. The Independent State of Samoa also has a number of newspapers, such as *Savali* and the *Samoa Observer*, produced by novelist Sano Malifa. There are also weekly magazines. Several Samoan newspapers appear in expatriate communities such as those in New Zealand. Local radio stations such as radio 2AP and state-run television are also important media in western Samoa.

index